Where is my life going?

GW00728150

STEPHEN HANCE

Jesus said: I came so they can have real and eternal life, more and better life than they ever dreamed of.

From the Bible, John chapter 10 verse 10,
The Message version

Contents

Everybody asks...

At some point, everyone wonders whether their life has a purpose.

Perhaps it's one of those questions that trouble us when we are unable to sleep at night. Maybe it's triggered by a joyful event, like the birth of a child. Or it could be triggered by something sad, like a divorce, or a scary diagnosis from the doctor. For some people, the question comes up when we finally achieve something we have dreamed of – that big promotion or the house we wanted to buy – and it feels good, but not quite as amazing as we had expected.

Many thinkers and writers have tackled this question.

Some say that our lives have no real purpose whatsoever. Atheist philosopher Jean-Paul Sartre wrote, 'Life has no meaning the moment you lose the illusion of being eternal.'

Others believe we create our own purpose for life. Author Jonathan Lockwood Huie has said, 'The meaning of life is whatever we choose.'

Some people argue that the goal of life is to succeed. Actor and politician Arnold Schwarzenegger says, 'The meaning of life is not simply to exist, to survive, but to move ahead, to go up, to achieve, to conquer.'

Meanwhile others suggest that the purpose of life is found in how we care for other people. The ancient Greek philosopher Aristotle wrote, 'What is the essence of life? To serve others and to do good.' And the Tibetan spiritual leader the Dalai Lama said, 'Our prime purpose in life is to help others.'

The trouble is, with so many answers to the question, how can we know what our lives are about? And what if we are wrong? What if we dedicate ourselves to success in our career, or building a healthy family, or service to others, and life still doesn't feel meaningful?

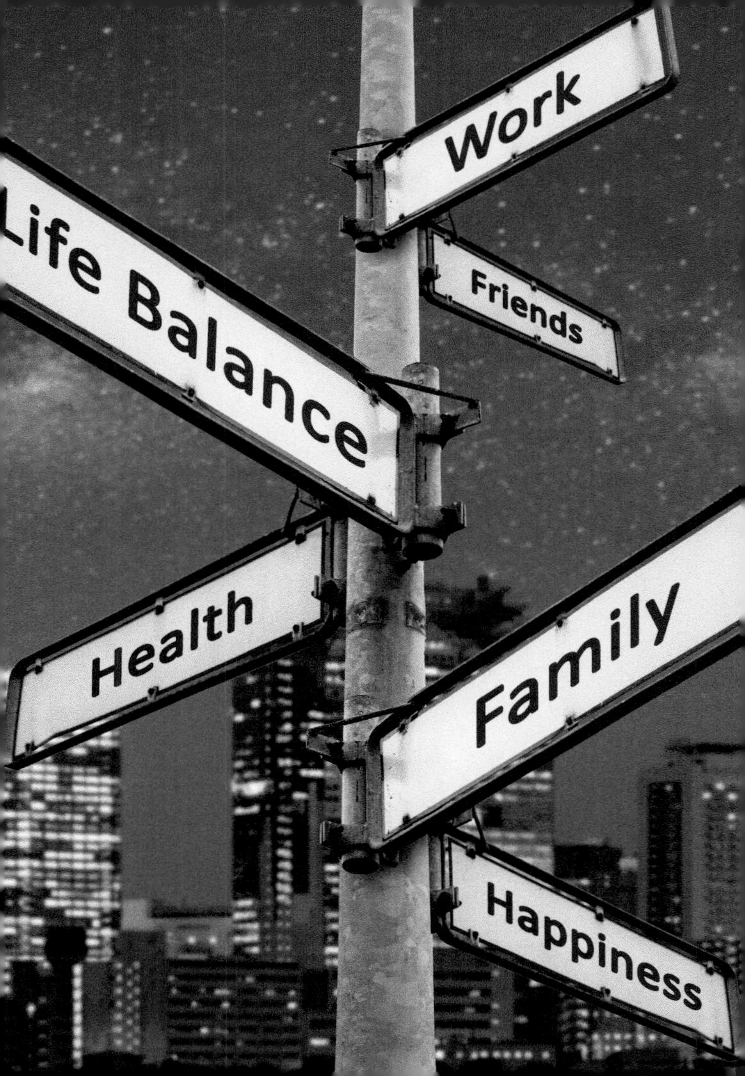
Work
Life Balance
Friends
Health
Family
Happiness

Christians believe...

Christians believe that life is not random or meaningless, but purposeful and significant. They also believe that the purpose of life cannot be found by looking deeper into ourselves but only by looking beyond ourselves. Our hopes and dreams for our lives matter, but they don't give us our ultimate purpose, although they may hint at it. Ultimate purpose can only be found by looking to God.

In 2002 a church leader in California wrote a book called 'The Purpose Driven Life'. Nobody was more surprised than the author, Rick Warren, when his book topped the best-seller lists across the USA and around the world. 'The Purpose Driven Life' went on to be translated into 137 languages and to sell more than 50 million copies, making it one of the best-selling non-fiction books of all time – testimony to the desire we all have, to find a purpose for our lives.

Warren's book begins with these words: 'It's not about you.' He goes on to explain that the only way we can discover purpose for ourselves is by looking to the one who created us. We don't expect a car or a washing machine to be able to tell us what they do and how they work. We expect the manufacturer to tell us this, through a user's guide or manual. In a similar way, only the God who made us can truly help us to find our purpose and our direction for life. Our purpose is discovered in relationship with God.

A much earlier Christian writer made the same point many years before. Augustine of Hippo lived in the 4th and 5th centuries AD in North Africa. Although his mother was a devout Christian, as a young man Augustine rejected her faith, and chose instead a lifestyle of pleasure and sexual indulgence. However, the faith of his childhood would not leave him alone. In his book 'Confessions', Augustine records that he used to pray, 'Lord, make me chaste [pure] – but not yet.' When finally Augustine committed his life to God, he at last found the sense of purpose for his life that had escaped him so far. He summed this up in the prayer, 'Lord, our hearts are restless, until they find their rest in you.'

Christians believe that this is a common human experience. Our hearts are restless. We look for purpose, for meaning, for happiness. We seek them in success, in relationships, in wealth, in experiences. And we enjoy these things, which can be very good in themselves. But our restlessness doesn't leave us. Only when we find our purpose in God can that restlessness find its fulfilment. And even then, it may be replaced by a different sort of restlessness. We will return to that idea later on.

In 1646 a gathering of church people produced a document called the Westminster Shorter Catechism. (A catechism is a teaching tool to help people learn and understand the Christian faith.) The Westminster Shorter Catechism was written as a series of questions and answers, because that is an easy way for us to take in and memorise information. The first question was, 'What is the chief end of man?' (meaning humanity, men and women alike). The answer is given that our 'chief end is to glorify God and enjoy him forever'.

This summarises what we have been saying. Christians believe that our ultimate purpose, the direction of a satisfying and meaningful life, is to know and love and follow God who has shown himself to us in Jesus.

So what about desire?

You might think at this point that I will want to contrast our restless longing for God with all the other desires and longings that we experience, and show those other desires to be unimportant or a distraction. Not a bit of it. All our best desires come from God and point to something that is God-given and that God wants to fulfil in us.

Let's think about some examples.

For some people, their sense of purpose is connected to their work. They experience a desire for their work which makes it

a kind of calling or vocation, not just something they do to pay the bills. They might take on a stressful job with low pay and long hours when they could choose to do something less demanding for greater reward. Challenges in their work which would exhaust many of us seem somehow to energise them. We might know people who work as teachers or in medicine who fit this description. But really this could be true of almost any kind of work. A manager is excited about getting the most out of her team. A scientist finds themselves unable to stop thinking about the theory they are testing, even when not at work. A farmer pictures what his fields will look like at harvest time and the people they will feed.

All these desires are God-given, as is the basic human impulse to work. Teachers share in the work of God to raise up the next generation and the compassion of Jesus who said, 'Let the little children come to me.' Nurses and doctors catch something of the desire of God to heal and make people whole. People who work for justice have a God-given vision to build a better world. Factory workers create things which make the lives of others easier. Great managers are inspired by God to help people to grow and thrive. And all healthy work reflects something of the nature of God, who made the universe, who saw that it was good, and who put a desire to be productive and creative into the human heart.

For other people, their sense of purpose or longing is connected with relationships. It might be the way a parent prioritises their family, taking joy in their children, and perhaps refusing a promotion that would require more time away from home. It could be the way someone has a real gift for friendship, building a community of people around them who might otherwise never meet, but come to care for one another. It could be the way that an adult child gently and lovingly cares for elderly parents who are becoming frail and confused. It could be in the longing that someone has for a partner, someone to know and love and share life with in the most intimate way.

All of these desires are God-given too. It was God who said of the first person named in the Bible 'It is not good for him to be alone.' It was God who gave us the capacity to love and the need to be loved by others. It was Jesus who taught that the person who loves also fulfils all the other commandments that God has given.

But we can go even further.

It's not just that our best desires are God-given or that those longings reflect something of what God is like. Christians believe that all of these are ultimately an expression of our longing for God.

Remember Augustine and 'Our hearts are restless until they find their rest in you'? This is what he was talking about.

We long for love and relationship with one another because those are wonderful things, but also because deep down we long to experience the love of God for ourselves.

We want to be creative because creativity is fulfilling and gives us a sense of meaning and value, but also because deep down we long to be like the creator God.

And that's why, even when we get what we think we want, the restlessness doesn't go away. We stop too soon. Our experience of human love is supposed to take us on into the love of God. Our experience of life-giving work and creativity is designed to lead us to God who creates all life. And so on.

CS Lewis, best known as the author of the Narnia books, wrote this in 'The Weight of Glory':

> *It would seem that Our Lord finds our desires not too strong, but too weak. We are half-hearted creatures, fooling about with drink and sex and ambition when infinite joy is offered us, like an ignorant child who wants to go on making mud pies in a slum because he cannot imagine what is meant by the offer of a holiday at the sea. We are far too easily pleased.*

We stop too soon.

But CS Lewis also makes this point in his book
'Mere Christianity'.

Creatures are not born with desires unless satisfaction for these desires exists. A baby feels hunger: well, there is such a thing as food. A duckling wants to swim: well, there is such a thing as water. Men feel sexual desire: well, there is such a thing as sex. If I find in myself a desire which no experience in this world can satisfy, the most probable explanation is that I was made for another world.

If our best desires are ultimately a longing for God, and if our desires imply that some satisfaction for that desire exists, then there must exist a God. And not just any old God, but a loving and personal God who can be known and experienced. And that is, of course, just what Christians believe to be true.

What did Jesus say?

Jesus spoke a lot about purpose and desire, about meaning and significance, about how to find joy and happiness. On one occasion he said this:

> *Whoever wants to save their life will lose it. But whoever loses their life for me will find it. What good is it if someone gains the whole world but loses their soul?*

From the Bible, Matthew chapter 16 verses 25-26a, New International Readers Version

Another time he said:

So don't worry. Don't say, 'What will we eat?' Or, 'What will we drink?' Or, 'What will we wear?' People who are ungodly run after all those things. Your Father who is in heaven knows that you need them. But put God's kingdom first. Do what he wants you to do. Then all those things will also be given to you.

From the Bible, Matthew chapter 6 verses 31-33, New International Readers Version

Jesus is not saying that our everyday concerns for our lives and the lives of those around us are wrong, nor that food and drink and clothing don't matter. What he seems to be saying is that if we focus firstly on God and receive all those good things as God's gift to us, then we will be in the best possible place. It is in giving ourselves to a cause bigger than ourselves that we find ourselves. It is in offering love and compassion to others that we receive love and compassion. It is in prioritising the Giver that we are free to enjoy his gifts to us.

Serving others

There are examples throughout history of Christians who have devoted their lives to serving others as an expression of their faith. Most go unnoticed by the wider world, but here are a few examples of people who have been recognised for their life and work.

The 18th century British politician and philanthropist, William Wilberforce was a leader of the movement to abolish the slave trade. In the same century Elizabeth Fry campaigned to reform prisons.

The Salvation Army, known around the world today for being one of the largest distributors of humanitarian aid, was founded by William and Catherine Booth to bring spiritual and practical help to those in need. They poured their energy into helping those trapped in poverty, homelessness, and addiction, and promoted equality for women. William Booth said:

While little children go hungry, as they do now, I'll fight. While men go to prison, in and out, in and out, as they do now, I'll fight. While there is a drunkard left, while there is a poor lost girl upon the streets, while there remains one dark soul without the light of God, I'll fight – I'll fight to the very end!

Nurse Edith Cavell was executed in 1915. She is celebrated for helping Allied soldiers escape from German-occupied Belgium during the First World War. Her Christian faith motivated her to save the lives of soldiers from both sides in the war, without discrimination. On the night before she died, she said:

Standing as I do in view of God and eternity, I realise that patriotism is not enough, I must have no hatred or bitterness towards anyone.

The British foodbank movement was begun by Carol and Paddy Henderson, who founded the Trussell Trust in 1997 as an expression of their Christian faith. John Kirkby founded CAP (Christians Against Poverty) in 1996. He believed God was calling him to give up his career in finance and use his knowledge of the industry to help the poor.

The Queen, who regularly mentions her Christian faith in her Christmas broadcasts to the Commonwealth, said in 2008:

I hope that, like me, you will be comforted by the example of Jesus of Nazareth who, often in circumstances of great adversity, managed to live an outgoing, unselfish and sacrificial life. Countless millions of people around the world continue to celebrate his birthday at Christmas, inspired by his teaching. He makes it clear that genuine human happiness and satisfaction lie more in giving than receiving; more in serving than in being served.

You could...

Finding purpose in life

What can you do if you would like to have a clearer sense of purpose, of direction in life? How can you find that for yourself? For many of us this is a life-long journey. But here are some suggestions that might help.

Think about yourself

Ask yourself some questions like this.

- What makes me tick?

- What do I care about?

- What am I good at?

- What gives me life and joy when I do it?

I remember once hearing a speaker talking about 'holy discontent' – the idea that some of us discover our purpose by recognising what really makes us angry or upset. It could be poverty, or neglect of children, or modern-day slavery.

Thinking about these questions should give us a good sense of the way we are made – our gifts and our passions, which are closely related to our purpose. You might want to ask one or two people who know you well what they think.

Of course, any self-help book might suggest something like this. But we don't stop there. Because this isn't just about trying harder on our own. The Bible is full of examples of God giving guidance, strength and encouragement to people.

Think about God and ask yourself some questions like this. (This is where it may get harder!)

- How can the things I've just thought about lead into an experience of God? For example, could my longing for love reflect my need to know God's love?

- What do the things I love and enjoy tell me about God?

- How might God be able to use the things I love and am good at to make things better, more in line with the way God wants the world to be? For example, if I volunteer in a charity shop, that could be a way of raising money to support some of the poorest people in the world.

Talk to God

Share your ideas with God and ask for his help. People of faith call this 'prayer' and it is really very simple. There is no need for clever phrases or special words. Talk to God the way you would talk to someone you trust – which is just who God is.

- Thank God for the special gifts and passions he has given to you.

- Ask God to help you use those gifts and passions to make the world a better place in some way.

- Ask God to show you how to do that and then sit quietly to listen. You never know what you might hear in return!

As you do this, not just once but in an ongoing way, you will capture more of a sense of who God made you to be, of how God sees you, and of the purpose God has for you to fulfil in the world. And then you will be happy and joyful, and the restlessness will be gone. Right?

Or perhaps not...

A new kind of restlessness

Many years ago, the Irish rock band U2 released their song 'I Still Haven't Found What I'm Looking For'. The lyrics describe various types of experience, even ecstasy, but then conclude each stanza, 'But I still haven't found what I'm looking for'.

Some members of U2 were known to be Christians, including singer and lyricist Bono. When the song came out, some people wondered whether he was renouncing his faith, moving on to look for something else. In interviews Bono made clear this was not the case. What Bono was looking for, as a Christian believer, was the promised time when the world would be at peace, when justice would reign, when hunger and hatred would end, when God would wipe away every tear.

YOUR JOURNEY STARTS HERE

When we open our lives to God and experience the work of God's Spirit, we begin to find our purpose. Our longings and desires make sense, as pointers to our calling in this world, and as pointers to the God who made us. With Augustine, we find our restlessness starts to ease. We begin to find our rest in God – and move forward as we share our life with him.

But if we stick with it, we might find a new kind of restlessness creeps in. And this is a God-provoked restlessness. It's a restlessness for God's kingdom of peace and justice. It's a restlessness for every person to know the love of God for themselves. It's a restlessness to find our purpose in seeing that kingdom come.

Notes

Explore more...

The website explorechristianity.info is a portal that can lead you to much more information. It will help you find answers from a Christian point of view to life's biggest questions.

You will find:

- Information about the Christian faith and its founder Jesus Christ

- Suggestions on how to begin living as a Christian

- Ideas to help faith grow

- Advice about meeting other Christians in churches and cathedrals

- Links to reliable websites where you can discover more.

explorechristianity.info

This is how much God loved the world: He gave his Son, his one and only Son. And this is why: so that no one need be destroyed; by believing in him, anyone can have a whole and lasting life. God didn't go to all the trouble of sending his Son merely to point an accusing finger, telling the world how bad it was. He came to help, to put the world right again.